THE INFANT

Oliver Lansley

THE INFANT

OBERON BOOKS
LONDON

WWW.OBERONBOOKS.COM

First published in 2011 by Oberon Books Ltd
Electronic edition published in 2012

Oberon Books Ltd
521 Caledonian Road, London N7 9RH
Tel: +44 (0) 20 7607 3637 / Fax: +44 (0) 20 7607 3629
e-mail: info@oberonbooks.com
www.oberonbooks.com

A catalogue record for this book is available from the British
Library.

PB ISBN: 978-1-84943-228-3
E ISBN: 978-1-84943-625-0

Cover design by Samuel Wyer

Introduction

The Infant was first produced in 2006 by my theatre company Les Enfants Terribles. Since then I have been fortunate enough to have seen several productions of the piece all over the world and I have, on separate occasions, produced, directed and performed in it.

I would say out of all my work *The Infant* is probably one of the most polarizing pieces. It makes some people mad! Throwing up question after question, who, what, why, where and when?

Some people love it, some people are frustrated by it, but usually people have an opinion one way or the other, which is great.

For me *The Infant* was always a play about questions, not about answers.

And so in this introduction I'm afraid I shall not be doing anything to shed any light on those questions. Your opinions are as valid as mine.

What I can say though is that the play is a reaction to hysteria and to the power of suggestion and fear. It's about manipulation, exploring what lengths people will go to if they feel their means are justified. It's about how easy it is for the consequences of an action to quickly overshadow the action itself and render it meaningless. How 'ends' can be forgotten whilst you're busy being caught up with the 'means'.

I don't think it was until I saw a production of the show in Italy, in Italian, that I finally realised the heart of the piece and my influences behind it. It is an absurdist play, influenced by the likes of Eugène Ionesco, Samuel Beckett and Harold Pinter. Seeing the piece performed in a language I didn't understand and with such a physical, European approach, it almost made more sense to me than seeing it played in English!

The key is to embrace its absurdity. That is after all the heart of its conceit.

However, saying that, life can always prove itself more absurd than anything one can conceive – as proved in February 2007, six months after the first production of this show, when news reports started circulating about a Muslim man in Birmingham who was allegedly arrested and questioned as a terrorist suspect over *'scribbles my kids had written in a diary'*.

It seems sometimes the truth really is stranger than fiction and that the more absurd an idea is, the more truth it can reveal.

I am thrilled after all these years to finally see *The Infant* published and hope that this will lead to many more questions and debates in years to come.

What is the picture? Who made it? And does it really matter?

Oliver Lansley

Characters

SAMEDI

CASTOGAN

COOPER

LILLY

The Infant was first premiered at The Billiard Room in The Gilded Balloon at the 2006 Edinburgh Fringe Festival. The production then transferred to The Old Red Lion in London.

The cast were:
SAMEDI – Alexander Gilmour
CASTOGAN – Graeme Brookes
COOPER – Simon Lee Phillips
LILLY – Pippa Duffy

Director – Jamie Harper
Designer – Signe Beckmann

A man, COOPER, sits on stage in a spotlight by a table, on the table sits a tape recorder. He is sitting on a chair with his arms tied behind his back, he has a black bag over his head, every now and then he struggles or makes a muffled noise.

Two smartly besuited men CASTOGAN and SAMEDI enter. CASTOGAN pulls off the man's hood and puts it onto the table. SAMEDI starts the tape recorder.

SAMEDI: Well well well what do we have here? Looks like we have a live one Castogan.

CASTOGAN: A live one? Oh me oh my they're my favourite type, live and kicking and biting at the bit.

CASTOGAN stares into the man's face, he kicks and squirms but is bound tightly.

CASTOGAN: My my my Samedi he is a spirited fellow.

SAMEDI: Isn't he just.

CASTOGAN: Squiggling like a little worm.

SAMEDI: Like a snake.

CASTOGAN: Or a weasel, like a ferret when you have him gripped tightly in your hands and he's wiggling and squirming all over the place trying to get out.

SAMEDI: Trying to get free.

CASTOGAN: Writhing and twisting.

SAMEDI: Like a ferret.

CASTOGAN: But we've got him gripped too tight.

SAMEDI: And he can't get free.

CASTOGAN: No.

SAMEDI: So he's just gonna wear himself out poor little fella.

The man stares at them and stops squirming.

CASTOGAN: He's stopped.

SAMEDI: Pray silence.

CASTOGAN: The penny has dropped

SAMEDI: The worm has turned.

COSTOGAN: Do you think he knows why he's here?

SAMEDI: I don't know, do you know why you're here?

The man stares at SAMEDI, still tightly gagged.

SAMEDI: It would seem not.

CASTOGAN: Well does he know who we are?

SAMEDI: Do you know who we are?

CASTOGAN: Oh my goodness how terrible, how impolite of us.

SAMEDI: It's shameful really.

CASTOGAN: Not to introduce ourselves, well my name is Castogan.

SAMEDI: And my name is Samedi…it's French for Saturday… the day on which God created man.

CASTOGAN: *(Preening himself.)* His greatest achievement some might say.

SAMEDI: Or his greatest failure might others say, it depends on how you look at it.

CASTOGAN: Or who is saying it, yes I suppose it does.

SAMEDI: So why is he here?

CASTOGAN: Well that's a good question.

SAMEDI: It is?

CASTOGAN: Yes.

SAMEDI: Thank you.

CASTOGAN: You're welcome.

SAMEDI: So what's the answer?

CASTOGAN: To what?

SAMEDI: The question?

CASTOGAN: What question?

SAMEDI: The good one.

CASTOGAN: Right the good one, what is the answer to the good question?

They both stop and look and the man.

SAMEDI: Do you think he knows?

CASTOGAN: He might do, *(To the man.)* do you know?... Seems not.

SAMEDI: Maybe he can't hear you.

CASTOGAN: *(Shouting.)* DO YOU KNOW?

SAMEDI: Maybe he's dumb.

CASTOGAN: *(Shouting.)* ARE YOU DUMB?...I don't think he knows.

SAMEDI: Maybe we've got the wrong guy.

CASTOGAN: The wrong guy, you think?

SAMEDI: Maybe.

CASTOGAN: My God that would be embarrassing.

SAMEDI: I might be wrong.

CASTOGAN: But so might he.

SAMEDI: That's true.

They both stare at him.

CASTOGAN: Do you think he can hear us?

SAMEDI: Yes.

CASTOGAN: Do you think he can understand what we're saying?

SAMEDI: Yes…

CASTOGAN: ENGLISH? DO YOU UNDERSTAND ENGLISH?

SAMEDI: Not much of a talker.

CASTOGAN: No.

SAMEDI: Maybe he's a mute.

CASTOGAN: Or a mime.

SAMEDI: Or a…maybe he's ignoring us.

CASTOGAN: Ignoring us why? Us? Why?

SAMEDI: I don't know.

CASTOGAN: You're not ignoring us are you? Why would he do that?

SAMEDI: Maybe he knows something we don't.

CASTOGAN: You think?

SAMEDI: Maybe.

CASTOGAN: Well what don't we know?

SAMEDI: I don't know.

CASTOGAN: Oh.

> *They stare at him.*

> *SAMEDI removes the man's gag.*

COOPER: Who are you? What do you want? What am I doing here? Help help please, somebody, help me?

CASTOGAN: He speaks.

SAMEDI: He's not dumb.

CASTOGAN: He has questions.

SAMEDI: Lots of them.

CASTOGAN: Which one do you think we should answer first?

SAMEDI: Well we already told him who we are.

CASTOGAN: He obviously wasn't listening.

COOPER: Please who are you? What do you want?

CASTOGAN: I'm Castogan.

SAMEDI: And I'm Samedi.

CASTOGAN: We told you this.

SAMEDI: French for Saturday remember?

COOPER: What do you want?

CASTOGAN: What do we want?

SAMEDI: What have you got?

COOPER: Please…

CASTOGAN: Please what?

COOPER: What do you want from me?

SAMEDI: What have you got for us?

COOPER: What are you talking about?

CASTOGAN: What we want.

COOPER: What?

SAMEDI: You asked us what we wanted, what do you have?

COOPER: What?

CASTOGAN: What? What? What?

SAMEDI: What are you keeping from us?

COOPER: Nothing.

CASTOGAN: Nothing?

SAMEDI: What are you hiding?

COOPER: Nothing.

CASTOGAN: Nothing?

SAMEDI: Liar.

CASTOGAN: LIAR!

COOPER: I'm not lying.

SAMEDI: First he asks us what we want then he tells us he's got nothing to give.

CASTOGAN: Cruel to dangle such a carrot.

SAMEDI: To toy with us like that.

CASTOGAN: Raise our expectations.

SAMEDI: Cruel.

CASTOGAN: Very.

COOPER: Who are you?

CASTOGAN: Again?

SAMEDI: We told you this…

CASTOGAN: Twice!

SAMEDI: I'm Castogan.

CASTOGAN: and I'm Samedi.

COOPER: But… I thought you were Castogan?

SAMEDI: I didn't think you knew who we were.

COOPER: But you said before…

CASTOGAN: Yes we did.

COOPER: So…which one's which?

SAMEDI: Well I'm…which one are you?

CASTOGAN: I thought I was Samedi.

SAMEDI: Really? See I thought I was Samedi, the whole, French for Saturday thing, the day…

CASTOGAN: Oh right God created man…his greatest achievement.

SAMEDI: …Or greatest failure right.

CASTOGAN: Right.

SAMEDI: Good.

CASTOGAN: Glad that's sorted.

Beat.

SAMEDI: Tea?

CASTOGAN: Please

SAMEDI: *(To COOPER.)* Tea?

COOPER: …I?

CASTOGAN: …I.

COOPER: …er

CASTOGAN: …er

SAMEDI: Jesus Christ man I'm only asking you if you'd like a cup of tea it's a simple question. Would you like a cup of tea?

COOPER: Yes.

CASTOGAN: Yes…?

COOPER: …please?

SAMEDI: Yes please, of course you can have a cup of tea, how do you take it?

CASTOGAN: Careful now.

COOPER: Milk and two.

SAMEDI: Milk and two? I take mine black.

CASTOGAN: Just milk for me.

SAMEDI: Just milk for him, I make the tea you see, he stews it dreadfully, nothing worse than a stewed cup of tea is there Castogan?

CASTOGAN: No Samedi.

SAMEDI: 2 – 3 minutes. That's how long it should be left to brew, isn't it Castogan?

CASTOGAN: Yes Samedi.

SAMEDI: Otherwise what happens?

CASTOGAN: Not long enough it's too weak, too long and it's stewed.

SAMEDI: Stewed! Indeed it is and there is nothing worse than a stewed cup of tea is there Castogan?

CASTOGAN: No Samedi.

SAMEDI: No… Right, well I shan't be long.

SAMEDI exits. CASTOGAN sits, lights a cigarette and pulls a small book from out of his pocket. He begins to read, paying no attention to COOPER. COOPER stares at him, waiting for something. There is a long beat. CASTOGAN smokes the entire cigarette then puts it out. SAMEDI re enters with tea.

SAMEDI: TEA.

CASTOGAN: TEA!

SAMEDI: Here we are…

SAMEDI stops.

SAMEDI: …have you been smoking?

CASTOGAN: No.

SAMEDI: Castogan?

CASTOGAN: I haven't.

SAMEDI: Castogan?

CASTOGAN: It was him.

SAMEDI: He was smoking?

CASTOGAN: Yes.

SAMEDI: With his arms tied behind his back?

CASTOGAN: Yes…

Beat.

SAMEDI: *(To COOPER.)* You really should quit you know. It'll kill you. Castogan used to smoke. I hated it. He doesn't do it any more.

They sit and drink their tea. Beat.

SAMEDI: *(To COOPER.)* You're not drinking your tea.

CASTOGAN: Is there something wrong with it?

SAMEDI: Milk and two just like you said.

CASTOGAN: Drink up.

COOPER: I can't.

SAMEDI: Can't?

COOPER: I'm tied up.

CASTOGAN: It didn't stop you from smoking.

SAMEDI: Tied up, of course you are how silly of me, how rude of us. Untie the man Castogan.

CASTOGAN: What?

SAMEDI: Untie the man.

CASTOGAN: But…

SAMEDI: Untie the man.

CASTOGAN: I…

SAMEDI: Castogan, he has to drink his tea for goodness sake. Untie the man.

CASTOGAN unsurely unties COOPER, COOPER looks anxious, he drinks his tea. CASTOGAN and SAMEDI watch him carefully.

CASTOGAN: Is it good?

COOPER: Yes.

SAMEDI: How you like it?

COOPER: Yes, thank you.

SAMEDI: You're welcome.

COOPER finishes his tea.

SAMEDI: Excellent… Re-tie him Castogan.

COOPER: But…

CASTOGAN re-ties him.

SAMEDI: Right well, enough of the small talk let's get down to business we all know why we're here.

COOPER: I don't.

SAMEDI: You do.

COOPER: I don't.

CASTOGAN: He's lying!

SAMEDI: Castogan…fetch it.

CASTOGAN: What?

SAMEDI: Fetch it.

CASTOGAN: I don't' want to.

SAMEDI: Fetch it!

CASTOGAN: Can't you, I don't want to touch it.

SAMEDI: For Salem's sake Castogan it can't hurt you.

CASTOGAN: But?

SAMEDI: Just fetch it!

CASTOGAN glares at COOPER then fetches a briefcase and opens it, he nervously pulls out a piece of paper and hands it to COOPER.

COOPER: What is it?

SAMEDI: You tell us.

COOPER: It's a picture.

CASTOGAN: Bingo.

COOPER: But what's it got to do with me?

SAMEDI: You tell us.

COOPER: I don't know.

CASTOGAN: Come on.

COOPER: It's a child's drawing, I don't know what…

CASTOGAN: A child's drawing?

SAMEDI: From the hand of a child?

CASTOGAN: Give me a break.

SAMEDI: You don't recognise it?

COOPER: No.

SAMEDI: Really?

COOPER: No I… *(He looks at it again, a spark of recognition flutters across his face.)* Is this…? Did my son draw this, is this…? If you've touched my son, if you've hurt my boy, if you've touched my son I'll kill you, I'll fucking kill you! Where is he? Where is he! YOU FUCKING BASTARDS I'LL FUCKING KILL YOU, I'LL KILL YOU.

CASTOGAN puts the gag back in COOPER's mouth.

SAMEDI: He seems to think his son did it?

CASTOGAN: Ridiculous.

SAMEDI: A child?

CASTOGAN: Pathetic, blaming a small child, his own son to try and get himself off the hook, it's disgusting.

SAMEDI: I didn't even know he had a son.

CASTOGAN: He probably hasn't, It's probably another lie.

SAMEDI: How old is your son?

COOPER tries to shout but cannot.

SAMEDI: Nod your head to tell us how old he is.

COOPER starts to nod, SAMEDI and CASTOGAN count the nods out loud as he does so.

SAMEDI & CASTOGAN: One…two…three…four…

CASTOGAN: Four?

SAMEDI: You're saying a four-year-old drew this?

CASTOGAN: Impossible.

SAMEDI: Incredible.

CASTOGAN: A four-year-old?

SAMEDI: Your son really drew this?

COOPER nods.

CASTOGAN: He's pathetic, pathetic.

SAMEDI ungags COOPER.

COOPER: Please what's going on, what is this about?

SAMEDI: You really don't know?

COOPER: No.

SAMEDI: You really don't understand?

COOPER: NO!

CASTOGAN: Liar! Tell us why you made the picture!

COOPER: I didn't.

CASTOGAN: LIAR!

SAMEDI: He doesn't know?

CASTOGAN: Bullshit!

COOPER: What? It's just a picture, a child's drawing.

CASTOGAN: JUST a picture.

SAMEDI: This 'picture' has made a lot of people nervous Mr.

COOPER: What?

CASTOGAN: You've upset a lot of people with this picture.

SAMEDI: A lot of people.

CASTOGAN: They're not happy.

SAMEDI: They're angry.

CASTOGAN: Furious.

SAMEDI: This is unacceptable.

COOPER: What? But it's just…

CASTOGAN: Did you really think you could get away with it?

COOPER: I…

SAMEDI: You've made a lot of people unhappy, they don't know how to feel.

CASTOGAN: Angry.

SAMEDI: Scared.

CASTOGAN: Confused.

SAMEDI: Threatened.

CASTOGAN: You're attacking these people.

SAMEDI: Their rights.

CASTOGAN: Their lives, their liberties.

SAMEDI: You're taking these from them.

CASTOGAN: Ripping these from them, stealing, abusing.

SAMEDI: You are hurting these people.

CASTOGAN: You are raping them.

SAMEDI: Destroying them and that is unacceptable.

CASTOGAN: *You* are unacceptable.

SAMEDI: What you have *done* is unacceptable.

CASTOGAN: And you must be punished.

SAMEDI: Castogan.

CASTOGAN: We demand vengeance.

SAMEDI: Castogan!

CASTOGAN: We are peaceful, we demand peace and you have taken it from us and so you must be destroyed!

SAMEDI: Castogan Christ calm it down, we're all civilised here, this isn't a witch hunt.

CASTOGAN: Then what is it?

SAMEDI: ...a trial?

COOPER: A trial?

SAMEDI: Everyone should be given a chance to prove their innocence.

CASTOGAN: Or guilt.

SAMEDI: Or guilt.

COOPER: I've done nothing wrong.

CASTOGAN: Liar!

COOPER: Please just let me go, I don't know what you're talking about. Who are these people? Who have I upset?

SAMEDI: Who haven't you upset?

CASTOGAN: You are the oppressor.

COOPER: You're not making any sense, I don't know what I've done.

Beat.

SAMEDI: You really don't understand?

COOPER: Honestly.

SAMEDI: And your son drew this picture?

COOPER: Yes but…

SAMEDI re-gags COOPER.

SAMEDI: We've got the wrong man.

CASTOGAN: What?

SAMEDI: He didn't make this.

CASTOGAN: What? You don't *believe* him?

SAMEDI: I believe him.

CASTOGAN: He's lying.

SAMEDI: I don't think so.

CASTOGAN: He's lying he knows exactly what he's doing.

SAMEDI: I don't think so.

CASTOGAN: Jesus come on he's our man. He's our man, he's the one who's done this...

SAMEDI: Look at him Castogan. Look at him, do you really see it in him?

CASTOGAN: Samedi he…

SAMEDI: He's not our man, Castogan. He's not our man.

CASTOGAN: But…

SAMEDI: He's not our man.

CASTOGAN slumps in frustration and puts his head in his hands, SAMEDI rests his hand on CASTOGAN's shoulder.

SAMEDI: I know, I know, we'll get him. We'll get him.

Beat.

SAMEDI, removes the gag and unties COOPER.

SAMEDI: I'm dreadfully sorry sir you're free to go.

COOPER: What?

SAMEDI: There's been a terrible mix up I can only apologise, please, you're free to go.

COOPER: Are you serious?

SAMEDI: Of course sir, please accept my sincerest apologies, I hope you do not feel too inconvenienced, I do hope you understand we were just doing our jobs.

COOPER: I…

SAMEDI: Castogan…

CASTOGAN ignores him.

SAMEDI: CASTOGAN!

CASTOGAN mumbles 'Sorry' sulkily under his breath.

SAMEDI: Thank you very much for your time sir.

COOPER: I can go now?

SAMEDI: Yes sir.

COOPER: Just like that?

SAMEDI: Yes sir.

COOPER: Just go?

SAMEDI: Yes sir.

COOPER stands there for a moment slightly dumbfounded, SAMEDI turns to CASTOGAN, they ignore COOPER.

SAMEDI: Come on Castogan cheer up.

CASTOGAN: I really thought that was him.

SAMEDI: Come on Castogan in your heart of hearts you must have known.

CASTOGAN: I just…

SAMEDI: It's the boy!…the boy…unbelievable, well I can honestly say I didn't see that one coming.

CASTOGAN: You really think it's him?

SAMEDI: Oh for sure.

CASTOGAN: Really?

SAMEDI: I'm positive.

CASTOGAN: Oh, well he should be easier to take care of, smaller, weaker.

SAMEDI: Don't be fooled Castogan.

COOPER: Excuse me?

SAMEDI: Oh hello sir can I help you?

COOPER: Sorry what were you talking about just then?

SAMEDI: What sir?

COOPER: Just then, you were talking about someone, a boy?

SAMEDI: It's private business sir, top secret I'm afraid we cannot discuss this with you.

COOPER: Were you talking about my boy?

SAMEDI: Sir we are not at liberty to...

COOPER: WERE YOU TALKING ABOUT MY SON?

CASTOGAN: Jesus Christ!

SAMEDI: Now sir would you please calm down.

COOPER: Calm down? I'm kidnapped, beaten, taken to some remote place, threatened, tortured, interrogated, intimidated...

SAMEDI: Sir as I have explained it was a misunderstanding...

COOPER: Misunderstanding?

CASTOGAN: Yes.

COOPER: Look, just tell me what this has got to do with me?

SAMEDI: Nothing!

COOPER: Then why am I here?

SAMEDI: I told you sir we made a mistake.

COOPER: What are you doing? What are you looking for?

CASTOGAN: Evil.

SAMEDI: Sir I've told you we are not at liberty to discuss this, all we can tell you is that we have eliminated you from our investigations and that you are free to go.

COOPER: So that's it?

SAMEDI: Yes.

COOPER: This was just a big mistake?

SAMEDI: Yes.

COOPER: And this has nothing to do with me?

SAMEDI: No.

COOPER: Or my son?

SAMEDI and COOPER look at each other, they do not answer.

COOPER: My son? This has got something to do with my son?

SAMEDI and CASTOGAN do not answer.

COOPER: Talk to me! What has this got to do with my boy?

SAMEDI: Sir your son is a serious threat to our national security.

COOPER: Serious threat? HE'S FOUR!

CASTOGAN: You've seen what he's capable of?

COOPER: What he's capable of? He's four, he can't spell his own name.

SAMEDI: I know it must be hard to come to terms with.

COOPER: Come to terms with?

CASTOGAN: He's a monster.

COOPER: What?

CASTOGAN: He's a menace, a danger to the very fabric of our society.

COOPER: What the hell are you talking about?

SAMEDI: Sir I think it's probably best if you leave.

COOPER: I'm not leaving!

SAMEDI: I think it would be best if…

COOPER: I'm not leaving, what are you talking about? What are you going to do to my son?

CASTOGAN: He must be stopped.

SAMEDI: Castogan.

CASTOGAN: He must be punished.

SAMEDI: CASTOGAN!

COOPER: Punished? He's a child.

SAMEDI: We were all children sir.

COOPER: Is this a joke? This is a joke right, it's a joke?

COSTOGAN: How dare you.

SAMEDI: Do we look like we're laughing sir?

COOPER: Please, please, what's happening? What do you want with my boy?

SAMEDI stands and thrusts the picture into COOPER's hands.

SAMEDI: Look at it.

COOPER: What?

SAMEDI: Look at it properly, what do you see?

COOPER: I don't know.

CASTOGAN: Try harder!

COOPER: I don't know…a man?

SAMEDI: What else?

CASTOGAN: What else do you see?

COOPER: I don't know, a…is that a tree? Or an umbrella?

CASTOGAN: Look harder.

SAMEDI: Look past it.

CASTOGAN: What does it mean?

SAMEDI: Look at it… Look at it.

CASTOGAN: Look at it…what do you see?

SAMEDI: What do you see…?

Blackout.

2.

CASTOGAN, SAMEDI and COOPER all sit in the room.

COOPER is sitting on the chair with his head in his hands weeping, CASTOGAN has his hand on his shoulder.

COOPER: No… NO!

CASTOGAN: Let it out.

COOPER: It's not possible.

SAMEDI: I know it's hard.

COOPER: Why?

CASTOGAN: No one can answer that.

COOPER: I just don't understand it, I don't know how it could have happened?

SAMEDI: You can't torture yourself over this.

COOPER: What have I done? What have I done? I've created a monster.

CASTOGAN: Now you mustn't blame yourself.

COOPER: I should have, I could have…

SAMEDI: There's no way you could have known.

CASTOGAN: These people hide it, they keep it from you, they don't want to be found out.

COOPER: All this time, how could I not have known, all those times I've held him, told him I loved him, all those times he's looked into my eyes and…

SAMEDI: There's nothing you could have done.

CASTOGAN: No way you could have known.

SAMEDI: It just happened.

CASTOGAN: And now we must make it right.

COOPER: Make it right?

CASTOGAN: Of course, you know the damage he could do, you've seen it with your own eyes.

COOPER: But…he's my son.

SAMEDI: You can't be emotional about these things.

CASTOGAN: He's not your son anymore.

COOPER: But maybe it was a mistake, perhaps he could…

SAMEDI: It's too late for that.

CASTOGAN: It's gone too far.

SAMEDI: It's too risky.

CASTOGAN: You've seen what he's capable of.

SAMEDI: Who knows how many he's already got following?

COOPER: Really?

CASTOGAN: Absolutely, that's how these people work, it's textbook.

COOPER: How could I not have known?

SAMEDI: They don't want to be found out, they're masters of disguise.

Beat.

COOPER: Now I think about it, it all starts to make sense.

CASTOGAN: There you go.

COOPER: The tantrums, the cold silences, he was never an easy child.

SAMEDI: No.

COOPER: He didn't sleep well, he used to refuse his food, sometimes he would just fly into a rage for no reason, kicking, screaming, shouting, crying.

SAMEDI: The signs are there,

CASTOGAN: psychopathic.

SAMEDI: Textbook.

COOPER: Then the next minute he'd be fine.

SAMEDI: They can just change.

CASTOGAN: Like a wild animal, you can keep it in your care for years, never see it act up then one day...

SAMEDI: Bang!

CASTOGAN: It's at your throat.

SAMEDI: It's teeth in your neck.

CASTOGAN: And by then it's too late.

COOPER picks up the picture and looks at it.

Beat.

CASTOGAN: You understand now?

COOPER: Yes...he must be stopped.

CASTOGAN: Destroyed. We will have peace if we have to kill every last one of them.

SAMEDI: All in good time, all in good time.

Beat.

COOPER: Do you think my wife's in on it too?

SAMEDI: It's possible.

CASTOGAN: Probable.

SAMEDI: We can't rule anything out.

COOPER: They're very close.

SAMEDI: I see.

COOPER: Always whispering and talking to each other.

CASTOGAN: Cell.

SAMEDI: Network.

COOPER: She's definitely changed since he came along. She's a different woman.

CASTOGAN: Textbook.

SAMEDI: It's amazing the power these people can wield.

CASTOGAN: The mask of power.

SAMEDI: You shouldn't see her as bad or stupid, just hungry and looking for food.

CASTOGAN: Wanting to believe.

SAMEDI: Weak.

CASTOGAN: We must take care of her too.

COOPER: Right.

SAMEDI: Are there others?

COOPER: Others?

SAMEDI: Associates? Partners?

COOPER: Well…he has a few friends.

CASTOGAN: They're breeding.

SAMEDI: It's natural.

CASTOGAN: We'll be busy.

COOPER: Do you really think…?

CASTOGAN: We can't take the chance.

SAMEDI: Best not to take the chance. We work for a higher power.

CASTOGAN: A greater good.

SAMEDI: You can't measure the lives of few against the lives of many.

CASTOGAN: To maintain peace we must prepare for war.

SAMEDI: Sacrifices must be made.

CASTOGAN: Collateral damage.

SAMEDI: Can't make an omelette with out breaking eggs.

COOPER: What happens next?

CASTOGAN: We bring in the boy.

SAMEDI: We must do what's right.

CASTOGAN: They want blood!

SAMEDI: They want *justice.*

CASTOGAN: Their thirst needs to be sated.

SAMEDI: Though that's not what this is about.

CASTOGAN: No?

SAMEDI: No.

CASTOGAN: Oh.

> *Beat.*

COOPER: …Do you think I could have another cup of tea?

SAMEDI: Of course, of course, yes, and maybe a slice of cake?

CASTOGAN: Cake?

SAMEDI: Yes Castogan.

CASTOGAN: Really?

SAMEDI: Yes…go on.

> *CASTOGAN jumps to his feet in excitement.*

SAMEDI: …and the tea?

CASTOGAN: 2 – 3 minutes.

SAMEDI: That's right.

CASTOGAN: No more no less.

SAMEDI: At a boy.

CASTOGAN: I won't be a minute.

SAMEDI: He loves his cake.

CASTOGAN runs out of the room.

COOPER smiles, SAMEDI stares at him grinning. Pause.

SAMEDI stares at COOPER, COOPER begins to feel uncomfortable. SAMEDI looks to check CASTOGAN has gone then reaches over and turns off the tape recorder, he swiftly moves over to COOPER loosening all his remaining ropes, checking he is ok, there is a change in him. He seems almost nervous.

SAMEDI: I can only apologise for this indignity I hope you understand, they are necessary measures.

COOPER: What?

SAMEDI: They're on to you…but we found you! It took us a while but we did! We found you, I've found you and here you are. May I say what an honour it…

COOPER: What are you talking about?

SAMEDI: A man of your vision…

COOPER: Please…

SAMEDI: I really admire what you've done…

COOPER: *(Confused.)* Excuse me?

SAMEDI: It's fantastic.

COOPER: What?

SAMEDI: You don't have to pretend, I get it… Really. I'm with you! For you, I'm… All this, it's a pretence… I needed to find you. I want to protect you.

COOPER: I don't understand.

SAMEDI: I mean obviously at first, I mean… I wasn't, not when I first heard about it, but when I saw it, saw it with my own eyes, when I saw it… You've opened my eyes, I think you're a genius.

COOPER: What are you talking about?

SAMEDI: The picture.

COOPER: The picture? My son's picture?

SAMEDI: Right your 'son's' picture… Brilliant! I can't believe he's fallen for it. He's a cretin.

COOPER: Who?

SAMEDI: Castogan, believing that a four-year-old could make such a thing.

COOPER: I but…

SAMEDI: How did you…? No don't tell me…

COOPER: Wait. The picture's bad. It's terrible I mean, what it means? What it says?

SAMEDI: Right, yes of course. Terrible…but brilliant.

COOPER: No.

SAMEDI: No? Sorry no, not brilliant…but so brave.

COOPER: Brave?

SAMEDI: No one else would say it but it's what we were all thinking.

COOPER: What?

SAMEDI: I'm sorry it's foolish of me to try and understand such a thing, I didn't mean to…all I'm saying is that I'm with you, you know? I'm on your side and the important thing is that we get you out of here.

COOPER: You can get me out?

SAMEDI: …Just keep doing what you're doing, play dumb. I'll take care of Castogan.

COOPER: Honestly I didn't…

SAMEDI: It'll change the world.

COOPER: You don't understand.

SAMEDI: I can smell it.

The door opens, CASTOGAN pops his head round the door.

CASTOGAN: Samedi could I have a word please?

SAMEDI: A word?

CASTOGAN: Yes.

SAMEDI: Of course, be right with you.

CASTOGAN closes the door, SAMEDI gets to his feet, he looks COOPER in the eye, stuffs the picture into his pocket. Gets up and exits.

3.

If possible have the set turn so that the interrogation room is now side on. We see the door that SAMEDI has just exited from, there is then a small corridor in which stands CASTOGAN and SAMEDI and then another wall leading to an identical interrogation room, which mirrors the first one. In here sits a woman, LILLY, beautiful, she looks nervous, she is dressed very primly. COOPER and LILLY sit in their separate rooms, anxiously. SAMEDI and CASTOGAN talk in the hallway. CASTOGAN holds a tray of tea and cake.

SAMEDI: What is it?

CASTOGAN: She's here.

SAMEDI: Who?

CASTOGAN: The wife.

SAMEDI: She's here?

CASTOGAN: Yes.

SAMEDI: Where?

CASTOGAN looks to the second interrogation room in which sits LILLY.

SAMEDI: Have you seen her?

CASTOGAN: Yes

SAMEDI: What's she like?

CASTOGAN: She's…pretty.

SAMEDI: Pretty Castogan? Pretty as a picture is she?

CASTOGAN: Yes.

SAMEDI: Keep your wits about you Castogan. Keep focused.

CASTOGAN: I am focused.

SAMEDI: Good then stay so. Have you spoken to her?

CASTOGAN: No.

SAMEDI: But you've seen her?

CASTOGAN: Yes... I looked through the little hole.

CASTOGAN references the door again. SAMEDI looks at him, then at the door. SAMEDI moves to the door and looks through the peephole. LILLY appears to look directly at him. He stays there for a long while. Then looks back to CASTOGAN.

SAMEDI: She is...pretty, I mean.

CASTOGAN: So what now?

SAMEDI looks at CASTOGAN for a moment.

4.

The scene is now set up like the first scene, except we are in LILLY's interrogation room as opposed to COOPER's.

LILLY sits there anxiously. The black hood that she was brought in wearing sits on the table. After a moment CASTOGAN and SAMEDI burst through the door.

CASTOGAN: TEA!

SAMEDI: Tea!

CASTOGAN: and Cake!

LILLY stares at them both confused.

LILLY: I...

SAMEDI: Is everything OK?

CASTOGAN: To your liking?

SAMEDI: ...are you happy?

CASTOGAN: Comfortable?

SAMEDI: Are you sitting comfortably?

CASTOGAN: Then we'll begin…

    CASTOGAN turns on the tape recorder.

LILLY: I'm sorry I, could somebody please just…

SAMEDI: My God I'm sorry.

CASTOGAN: We're sorry.

SAMEDI: We've done it again.

CASTOGAN: How terribly rude.

SAMEDI: Frightfully.

CASTOGAN: Not to introduce ourselves, my name is Castogan.

SAMEDI: And my name is Samedi…it's French for Saturday… the day on which God created man.

CASTOGAN: His greatest achievement.

SAMEDI: Or his greatest failure, dependant on how you look at it.

CASTOGAN: Yes.

SAMEDI: So that's us but what about you?

CASTOGAN: Let's talk about you.

LILLY: Please could somebody just tell me…

SAMEDI: *(Cutting her off.)* Ah ah ah ah ah, name first?

LILLY: What?

CASTOGAN: Your name?

LILLY: My name is Lilly.

SAMEDI: Lilly how lovely.

CASTOGAN: How delightful.

SAMEDI: Like the flower.

CASTOGAN: Yes like the flower, you're like the flower.

LILLY: Please…

SAMEDI: Lilly do you know why you're here?

LILLY: No.

CASTOGAN: Are you sure?

LILLY: Yes.

SAMEDI: Think very hard Lilly.

CASTOGAN: As hard as you can.

LILLY: I DON'T KNOW! *(Starting to get upset.)*

SAMEDI: You've upset her now.

CASTOGAN: I didn't mean to…it wasn't…

SAMEDI: Apologise to Lilly.

CASTOGAN: I'm sorry Lilly I really am.

SAMEDI: He didn't mean to upset you.

CASTOGAN: I really didn't.

LILLY: What do you want?

CASTOGAN: Aw she's lovely, you're lovely.

SAMEDI: Castogan.

CASTOGAN: Look at her wrinkling her nose up…all stern.

SAMEDI: Castogan!

SAMEDI stares at CASTOGAN for a second, CASTOGAN looks at SAMEDI. Beat.

SAMEDI: Goodness the tea, the tea's getting cold.

CASTOGAN: The tea is getting cold.

SAMEDI: Lilly how do you take it?

CASTOGAN: The tea, Lilly he means the tea.

SAMEDI: I do.

LILLY: …just milk please.

SAMEDI: Just milk.

CASTOGAN: Because you're sweet enough.

SAMEDI: Cake?

CASTOGAN: Cake Lilly… Oh and what cake!

SAMEDI: He loves his cake!

CASTOGAN: I do.

SAMEDI puts the tea and a slice of cake on the table in front of LILLY, she stares at them.

SAMEDI: So…

CASTOGAN: So…

They both stare at her for a moment, she stares back.

SAMEDI goes to speak, then stops. Beat.

SAMEDI: …Where's the picture?

CASTOGAN: The picture? I left it with you.

SAMEDI: With me? I don't have it.

CASTOGAN: Then where is it?

SAMEDI: I don't know.

CASTOGAN: Well *I* don't know

SAMEDI: Well where was it?

CASTOGAN: With you…and him.

SAMEDI: You mean it's with him?

CASTOGAN: …well, no, maybe… I left it with you.

SAMEDI: But now it's with him, great Castogan, great!

CASTOGAN: But I didn't…

SAMEDI: Perfect!

CASTOGAN: But…

SAMEDI: Well I best go fetch it eh Castogan…? Providing he hasn't destroyed it already! Destroyed the evidence!

CASTOGAN: What? No he…he can't, he wouldn't…

SAMEDI sighs, jumps to his feet and walks out of the door.

CASTOGAN: He wouldn't…would he?

CASTOGAN looks back to LILLY who is staring at him desperately. They stare at each other for a beat. CASTOGAN is on edge. Beat.

CASTOGAN pulls out a cigarette and puts it in his mouth. He offers one to LILLY, she declines, he sparks up and smokes.

There is a long pause, CASTOGAN stares at LILLY, she is uncomfortable.

CASTOGAN: Don't you worry. It'll all be over soon, we'll sort it out.

He smiles at her. She looks at him. He looks around conspiratorially, he turns off the tape recorder. Then leans in and whispers to her.

CASTOGAN: I know it wasn't you… I can tell. You're not the type.

LILLY: Please, just tell me what's going on.

He looks at her sympathetically. After a beat he breaks, he continues to whisper.

CASTOGAN: Look I shouldn't really say anything. Technically you're a prisoner and…

LILLY: A prisoner?

CASTOGAN: It's about the picture.

LILLY: Picture? What picture?

CASTOGAN: Your son.

LILLY: *(Starting to panic.)* My son? My son? What's this got to do with my son? Is he OK? Where is he? What's happened to him?

CASTOGAN eyes her sympathetically.

CASTOGAN: We have reason to believe your son is engaged in terrorist activity.

LILLY: *(Flabbergasted.)* What?

CASTOGAN: That he is an enemy of the state.

LILLY: He's four!!

CASTOGAN: I know it's hard for you to comprehend.

LILLY: He's a four-year-old boy.

CASTOGAN: He is a danger to our very way of life! A threat to our civil liberties, an opponent of democracy, an ally of evil, a fly in our ointment, an enemy within, a sleeper, a militant, a guerilla, a menace, he is one of the horsemen, one of 'them', he wants to destroy 'us' and it may already be too late…

Lilly, may I call you Lilly? To your knowledge does your son have connections to any known terrorist organisations?

LILLY stares at him flabbergasted.

Has he ever done business in the Middle East, or with the Russians, or the Chinese, or the Koreans, South Koreans, Iraqis, Iranis whatever the hell you call them, does he speak Spanish? French? Has he ever been to Colombia? Does he wear flat-heeled shoes? Does he have any frequent flyer miles? Does he ever spend long amounts of time inexplicably visiting government buildings? Does he pray or worship anyone or anything? Has he ever been to Germany? Has he ever attended any sort of protest? Is he a member of any club, group, organisation, institute, establishment, foundation, society? How does he feel about the Jews? Does he contribute regularly to any charity? Does he have any offspring you don't know about? Does he read any of 'the political' newspapers? Has he ever taken flying lessons? Does he look good in orange? Has he ever been on a pilgrimage? Has Jesus saved him? Has he even been to 'Mecca'? Can he build a bomb? Did you ever drop him as a child? Does he at times seem cold and distant? Does he own a computer? Do his hands get clammy when he watches the news? Does he lock the door when goes to the bathroom? Does he lie to you for no reason? Do his eyes look dead when he tells you he loves you? Does he love you Lilly? Really? Can you be sure of it? Would you be willing to swear it in a court of law?

Suddenly we hear COOPER scream with pain from the other room they both look up anxiously.

LILLY: What was that?

CASTOGAN: It sounded like a scream

LILLY: Who was it? It sounded like my husband?

CASTOGAN: You're married?

LILLY: My husband? What are you doing to him? COOPER?
COOPER?

CASTOGAN: Oh him right of course…*he's* your husband of
course he is!

LILLY: Please what are you doing to him?

*They hear a door close, CASTOGAN panics, puts out the cigarette
and waves the air.*

CASTOGAN: Look when Samedi gets back I didn't say
anything right?

LILLY: What?

CASTOGAN: I didn't tell you anything, about your son, about
the picture nothing.

The door starts to open.

CASTOGAN: *(Spitting it out.)* And I wasn't smoking!

CASTOGAN turns the tape recorder back on.

SAMEDI enters with the picture.

SAMEDI: Right so here we are…

CASTOGAN: What took you so long?

SAMEDI: I…has somebody been smoking?

*SAMEDI looks at CASTOGAN and LILLY, they both look up at him
anxiously.*

SAMEDI: It smells of smoke, has someone been smoking?

CASTOGAN: No…

SAMEDI: Castogan?

SAMEDI sniffs the air, then stares at LILLY.

CASTOGAN: Fine I had a cigarette!

SAMEDI: CASTOGAN!

CASTOGAN: Just one!

*SAMEDI grabs CASTOGAN by the lapels goes and puts his face right
up against his, he spits out the words.*

SAMEDI: Castogan, formaldehyde, ammonia, hydrogen sulfide are all now working on the sensitive membranes of your eyes, nose and throat, irritating them and producing abnormal thickening in the membranes lining your gullet. *(SAMEDI prods him in the chest.)* A layer of sticky cancer producing tar is now being deposited on the lining of your throat and bronchi and the free-roving scavenger cells that remove foreign particles from the delicate air sacs of your lungs are gradually being weakened. These gases are also causing chemical injury to the tissues of your lungs, speeding up the production of mucus and leading to an increased tendency to cough up sputum...

SAMEDI slaps him on the back, CASTOGAN coughs.

...this excess mucus is a breeding ground for a wide variety of bacteria and viruses, making you more susceptible to colds, flu, bronchitis and other respiratory infections. And if you do come down with an infection, your body will be less able to fight it, because smoking impairs the ability of the white blood cells to resist invading organisms.

SAMEDI grabs CASTOGAN's wrist.

...your pulse has quickened, your heart is being forced to work harder, to beat an extra ten to 25 times per minute, increasing your risk of heart attack, stroke and vascular disease of the extremities which in severe cases may require amputation. Your sperm count is decreasing, as is your sperm mobility and sperm shape and you may start to suffer erectile problems...

That one cigarette Castogan has cost you five to 20 minutes of your precious life... You may need those extra five minutes Castogan, you may have something very important you wish to do, or say and now. *(SAMEDI clicks his fingers.)* They're gone. Think about that next time Castogan, think about it.

CASTOGAN sits there terrified, SAMEDI turns back to LILLY, bright as if nothing has happened and puts the picture onto the table.

SAMEDI: So Lilly...about this picture.

Blackout.

5.

We see the two interrogation rooms side on.

SAMEDI: …Where is the picture?

CASTOGAN: The picture? I left it with you.

SAMEDI: With me? I don't have it.

CASTOGAN: Then where is it?

SAMEDI: I don't know.

CASTOGAN: Well *I* don't know.

SAMEDI: Well where was it?

CASTOGAN: With you…and him.

SAMEDI: You mean it's with him?

CASTOGAN: …well, no, maybe… I left it with you.

SAMEDI: But now it's with him, great Castogan, great.

CASTOGAN: But I didn't…

SAMEDI: Perfect!

CASTOGAN: But…

SAMEDI: Well I best go fetch it eh Castogan…? Providing he hasn't destroyed it already! Destroyed the evidence!

CASTOGAN: What? No he…he can't, he wouldn't…

SAMEDI sighs, jumps to his feet and walks out of the door.

CASTOGAN: He wouldn't…would he?

Inside the interrogation room CASTOGAN looks back to LILLY who is staring at him desperately. They stare at each other for a beat. CASTOGAN is on edge. Beat. CASTOGAN pulls out a cigarette and puts it in his mouth. He offers one to LILLY, she declines, he sparks up and smokes.

Meanwhile in the hallway SAMEDI stands, almost catching his breath, he pulls the picture from out of his pocket and stares at it, his hands almost shaking. After a long beat, he moves to the spyhole

*of the room where CASTOGAN and LILLY sit and stares through it.
He then looks back to the picture, then runs over to the spyhole on
the door to COOPER's room and watches through there. COOPER
sits anxious and confused. SAMEDI looks back to the picture. Grips
it tightly almost psyching himself up, then enters COOPER's room.*

6.

*Back in the first interrogation room, COOPER sits there alone, trying to
figure things out. SAMEDI enters.*

SAMEDI: Look we don't have much time…

COOPER: Why are you…?

SAMEDI: This picture! Cooper, this picture has changed my
life, you do not understand what I am sacrificing by just
talking to you. I see it, I see what you're trying to do.

COOPER: I didn't make the picture.

SAMEDI: …I applaud you.

COOPER: What do you want from me?

SAMEDI: Just a seat at the table. You're a prophet, a saviour,
we can't let this be swept under the rug, you are too
important…

SAMEDI looks around him conspiratorially.

SAMEDI: I will get you out of this, you just have to do exactly
what I say?

COOPER stares at him.

COOPER: Please…get me out of here.

SAMEDI stares at him. He puts his hand on his shoulder.

SAMEDI: Look, Castogan, the dolt, he believes that your son
drew the picture, if we play this right, we can let him take
the fall.

COOPER: Castogan?

SAMEDI: Your son.

COOPER goes to speak but SAMEDI stops him.

SAMEDI: I understand.

COOPER: My son?

SAMEDI: We have your wife.

COOPER: What?

SAMEDI: She's in the room next door, how much does she know?

COOPER: What? Lilly? Nothing, she doesn't know anything.

SAMEDI: Perfect. We can pin it on them, her and the boy.

COOPER: No wait.

SAMEDI: You had no idea what was going on, it was all their doing, conspiring behind your back. We let them take the fall. We get you out, you go underground, you do whatever you have to do? You understand?

COOPER: Take the fall? What do you mean?

SAMEDI grabs the picture.

SAMEDI: This is treason, Cooper, high treason, you understand how big this is. You'll be lucky to get away with the death penalty.

COOPER: What?

SAMEDI: They will kill you, destroy you, make an example of you.

COOPER: No, please, I'm innocent!

SAMEDI: Unless you let them take the fall... I can get you out of this.

COOPER: ...You mean sacrifice my son?

SAMEDI: And your wife to save yourself yes. Necessary measures. Can't make an omelette Cooper, can't make an Omelette, think about the cause.

COOPER sits back for a moment trying to take it in.

SAMEDI: *(Changing tact.)* The boy is a threat to you Cooper, as is his mother. He'll want to kill you, replace you, it's in his genes, it's proven, textbook, that's what they do. It's natural... Personally I don't see the tragedy in a father outliving their son.

Beat.

SAMEDI: It's you or them Cooper, you have to prioritise, decide who is more important, and I think you know the answer to that my friend. This! *(Holding the picture in front of him.)* THIS is what they will die for, for a cause...it won't be in vain, they will be martyrs, we can make them saints.

COOPER: ...I don't want to die.

SAMEDI: Of course you don't Cooper.

COOPER: What do I have to do?

SAMEDI: Nothing, I'll do all the work, you just...play dumb.

SAMEDI looks at his watch.

SAMEDI: I've been in here too long, they'll start to get suspicious.

SAMEDI looks around, he then lifts his foot and stamps on COOPER's toe, COOPER howls with pain.

SAMEDI: Sorry, necessary measures.

A moment later we hear LILLY shout 'COOPER, COOPER!'

COOPER: Lilly?

SAMEDI: Don't you worry sir, I'll take care of her.

SAMEDI jumps to his feet, takes the picture and exits.

Blackout.

7.

We are back in the interrogation room with LILLY and SAMEDI and CASTOGAN, LILLY is staring at the picture, baffled. She has been crying, CASTOGAN stands next to her with a box of tissues.

LILLY: ...It just all seems so surreal.

CASTOGAN: I know it must be hard to take in.

LILLY: How could he... He's so young.

SAMEDI: They are these days?

SAMEDI takes the picture, sits and looks at it, ignoring LILLY. LILLY watches him helplessly, then looks up to CASTOGAN.

LILLY: ...Please, he's just a child, he can't have done this.

CASTOGAN: I'm sorry.

LILLY: There must be another explanation.

SAMEDI: There isn't.

LILLY: But maybe you've made a mistake.

SAMEDI: We haven't.

LILLY: He's not capable of this, I know, please you have to believe me.

SAMEDI: I'm sorry but the facts speak for themselves.

LILLY looks devastated, she doesn't know what to say. CASTOGAN stares at her sympathetically. He then looks to SAMEDI.

CASTOGAN: Maybe she's right Samedi.

SAMEDI: What?

CASTOGAN: I mean it does seem a bit much for a child.

SAMEDI: Castogan we've been through this.

CASTOGAN: I know it just seems so hard to believe.

SAMEDI: Castogan.

LILLY: Did Cooper know about this?

SAMEDI: No

CASTOGAN: He denies it... But he could be hiding something.

SAMEDI: He's not.

CASTOGAN: He could be trying to cover for himself.

LILLY: Really?

SAMEDI: No.

CASTOGAN: *(Thinking.)* ...He did say he thought that you might be involved.

LILLY: What?

SAMEDI: Well...

CASTOGAN: He said that you could have been in on it.

LILLY: *(Taken aback.)* …He said that?

SAMEDI: …He said that you and the boy were very close.

LILLY: He's my son.

CASTOGAN: Abnormally close, always whispering and talking to each other.

LILLY: That's ludicrous.

CASTOGAN: He said you'd changed since the boy came along… 'She's a different woman.' That's what he said.

LILLY: I don't believe it.

SAMEDI: It's true.

CASTOGAN: It's true Lilly it is…you're too good for him.

Beat, LILLY considers.

LILLY: …He really thinks I'm part of this…conspiracy?

SAMEDI: Network.

CASTOGAN: Cell.

SAMEDI: …Yes.

LILLY: …Well he's lying!

CASTOGAN: I knew it!

LILLY: …If anyone's part of it it's him.

CASTOGAN: Of course it is.

LILLY: He's the boy's father, he looks up to him, worships him, emulates him.

CASTOGAN: Right.

LILLY: Anything my son did or drew or thinks is because of him. He's the one behind all this.

CASTOGAN: Yes, YES!!

SAMEDI: Hang on.

CASTOGAN: …playing us like a cheap tin whistle.

LILLY: Lying to me all this time.

CASTOGAN: Us, lying to us.

LILLY: Pulling the wool over my eyes.

CASTOGAN: A wolf in sheep's clothing.

SAMEDI: Wait!

LILLY: All these years…

CASTOGAN: You poor thing, you poor sweet creature.

LILLY: I didn't know.

CASTOGAN: Of course you didn't.

LILLY: I loved him.

CASTOGAN: *loved.*

LILLY: My son couldn't have done this.

CASTOGAN: That's what I said!

LILLY: *He* must have done this, done this to him.

CASTOGAN: It's the only explanation.

LILLY: To my little boy…

CASTOGAN: He's the innocent in all this.

LILLY: Why would he…?

CASTOGAN: Why, why? why? There is no why?

LILLY: He's just a child…

CASTOGAN: We'll stop him Lilly, we'll get him, we'll make him pay.

CASTOGAN goes to storm out to COOPER's room. SAMEDI stops him.

SAMEDI: Now just hold on for one second. Maybe your son has manipulated your husband in the same way that he manipulated you.

LILLY: What?

CASTOGAN: You're positive that you know nothing about this picture?

LILLY: Yes. No, nothing.

SAMEDI: Then perhaps he knows nothing too, perhaps he's telling the truth.

CASTOGAN: Samedi, you heard what Lilly said, she said that he was behind it.

SAMEDI: I heard her.

CASTOGAN: That the boy worships him, emulates him…

SAMEDI: I heard what she said Castogan.

LILLY: My son couldn't have done this.

SAMEDI: It's natural for a mother to be protective of her child but we have to be open to the possibility of…

CASTOGAN: Are you calling her a liar?

SAMEDI: Don't you take that tone with me Castogan.

CASTOGAN: He's been lying to us this whole time Samedi, he's toying with us. Taking us for fools.

SAMEDI: CASTOGAN!

CASTOGAN: I'm just saying… It's textbook. He's setting the boy up to take the fall. We don't want the hammer, we want the hand.

SAMEDI takes a moment. He stands and paces then turns back to LILLY.

SAMEDI: You do understand what this is don't you miss? What you're accusing your husband of? It's treason, high treason. He'll be executed, at best. You understand that?

LILLY doesn't answer.

SAMEDI: Do you understand that?

CASTOGAN: She understands.

SAMEDI: And you maintain that you are the innocent in all this.

LILLY: …and my son.

CASTOGAN: Her son is just a pawn, *(Nodding to the door.)* it's him we want.

SAMEDI glares at CASTOGAN.

SAMEDI: ...And you maintain this stance?

LILLY: ...Yes.

Beat.

SAMEDI: You have reason to believe that your husband is behind this picture?

LILLY: Yes.

SAMEDI: ...and you would be willing to swear that in a court of law?

LILLY leans forward and looks SAMEDI clean in the eye.

LILLY: ...I would swear it to my very grave.

Beat.

SAMEDI: I see...

SAMEDI looks at CASTOGAN. He paces for a moment. He then looks at CASTOGAN and nods to the door, he then turns off the tape recorder. CASTOGAN gives a friendly look to LILLY then stands and exits with SAMEDI.

8.

We see the set-up from side on again, LILLY and COOPER sit in their respective rooms. CASTOGAN and SAMEDI stand in the small corridor separating the two rooms. SAMEDI thinks, CASTOGAN seems to have made up his mind.

CASTOGAN: It's cut and shut.

SAMEDI: I don't believe her.

CASTOGAN: What?

SAMEDI: She's lying.

CASTOGAN: No she can't be, you're wrong.

SAMEDI: I'm not wrong Castogan, she's a liar.

CASTOGAN: NO! SHE'S...

SAMEDI: CASTOGAN!

SAMEDI grabs CASTOGAN by the lapels, CASTOGAN eyeballs him. COOPER and LILLY react to the shouting outside the doors.

SAMEDI and CASTOGAN remain static for a moment, SAMEDI releases his grip.

SAMEDI and CASTOGAN look to the respective doors.

SAMEDI: Bring her in.

CASTOGAN: What?

SAMEDI: Bring her in.

They look at each other, keeping their eyes on one another SAMEDI slowly moves into COOPER's room, CASTOGAN moves to LILLY's, they watch each other closely, then the moment the door closes SAMEDI rushes to COOPER and CASTOGAN to LILLY.

SAMEDI: I'm bringing in your wife.

COOPER: What?

CASTOGAN: I'm taking you to your husband.

LILLY: What?

SAMEDI: She's insisting it's you.

LILLY: I don't want to see him.

COOPER: She's blaming me?

CASTOGAN: Don't worry.

SAMEDI: I will get you out of this.

CASTOGAN: We can get through this.

SAMEDI: Just stay focused.

CASTOGAN: Remain calm.

SAMEDI: Deny everything.

CASTOGAN: Tell the truth.

SAMEDI: Play dumb.

CASTOGAN: Trust me.

SAMEDI: Trust me.

CASTOGAN: I won't let anyone hurt you Lilly.

SAMEDI: I will get you out of this Cooper.

CASTOGAN: Don't be intimidated by him.

SAMEDI: Forget about her.

CASTOGAN: You have to let him go.

SAMEDI: Necessary measures.

CASTOGAN: The truth will set you free.

SAMEDI: I can help you.

CASTOGAN: Let me help you.

COOPER: Help me.

LILLY: Please, help me.

SAMEDI and CASTOGAN put their hands on COOPER and LILLY's shoulders.

Blackout.

9

We are now in one of the interrogation rooms.

LILLY and COOPER sit next to each other, they look very uncomfortable. SAMEDI and CASTOGAN watch them, SAMEDI eyeing LILLY, CASTOGAN eyeing COOPER. They then switch, SAMEDI giving COOPER a look, CASTOGAN giving LILLY a look.

After a moment SAMEDI turns on the tape recorder. Throughout the first part of this scene SAMEDI and CASTOGAN direct their inquisition towards LILLY and COOPER respectively.

SAMEDI: We have reason to believe that someone is planning something…

CASTOGAN: Something big.

SAMEDI: That they are a significant threat to our existence.

CASTOGAN: Our civil liberties.

SAMEDI: Our way of life.

COOPER and LILLY look at one another.

SAMEDI: Exhibit A.

SAMEDI holds his hand out to CASTOGAN, who hands him the picture.

CASTOGAN: Exhibit A.

SAMEDI: Exhibit A. This picture, this image that has caused such a stir.

CASTOGAN: Such a fuss.

SAMEDI: That has got so many people worried

CASTOGAN: Upset.

SAMEDI: Angry.

CASTOGAN: *(Confronting COOPER.)* What does it mean?

SAMEDI puts his hand on CASTOGAN's shoulder as if to calm him down.

SAMEDI: Yes what does it actually mean? What is the extent of this plan?

CASTOGAN continues to glare at COOPER. SAMEDI looks at him.

SAMEDI: Castogan. Would you please fetch exhibit B.

CASTOGAN shoots COOPER another look, he then looks to LILLY supportively and exits, SAMEDI watches him leave then eyeballs COOPER and LILLY.

Moments later CASTOGAN returns with a child's toy, perhaps some sort of toy gun.

CASTOGAN: Exhibit B.

SAMEDI: Exhibit B!

CASTOGAN: Exhibit B was taken from the subject's living quarters.

COOPER: What?

LILLY: Our house? You've been in our house?

SAMEDI: Exhibit B appears to be some sort of electronic weapon, its exact function is unconfirmed but on some packaging recovered from the scene it claims to emit 'realistic laser light and sound action.'

LILLY: It's a toy for Christ's sake!

SAMEDI eyeballs LILLY.

SAMEDI: You recognise this then Lilly?

LILLY: Yes it's a toy, a stupid toy we bought it for our son.

SAMEDI: You bought it for him. Why would you buy your four-year-old son a weapon Lilly?

LILLY: It's not real.

CASTOGAN: She said 'WE', we bought it. You're the breadwinner aren't you Cooper? The man of the house, the provider, it was your money wasn't it Cooper? You bought this, you bought this thing, didn't you?!

COOPER: I've never seen it before!

LILLY: What? You're lying!

CASTOGAN: Liar!

SAMEDI: Fetch exhibit C.

CASTOGAN exits, moments later he returns with another childs toy, this time it is some sort of building.

CASTOGAN: Exhibit C.

SAMEDI: Exhibit C appears to be a scaled-down model of a building probably to be used as a type of schematic to plot some sort of attack or siege. The actual building the model is based on is as yet unknown.

LILLY: This is ridiculous.

SAMEDI: You better start taking this seriously you're in a lot of trouble.

LILLY: Castogan?

SAMEDI: Castogan?

CASTOGAN: What is it Cooper? The building? What are you planning?

COOPER: I don't know what you're talking about. Please, Samedi?

CASTOGAN: SAMEDI!?

SAMEDI: CASTOGAN! Fetch Exhibit D?

CASTOGAN sighs, exits and re-enters with a children's book.

CASTOGAN: Exhibit D.

SAMEDI: Exhibit D, a book entitled 'Humpty Dumpty'
thought to be a political allegory suggesting 'the great fall'
of civilised society and the establishment's inability to
'put it back together again', various other items of similar
propaganda were recovered from the subject's possessions.

CASTOGAN: Do you know the story Cooper?

SAMEDI: Did you read him this story Lilly?

LILLY: This is…it doesn't mean anything.

SAMEDI: It means everything Lilly.

LILLY: It's a children's story, a story about an egg.

SAMEDI: No it's a story about breaking eggs.

SAMEDI stares at LILLY and COOPER.

Beat.

SAMEDI: All of this is irrefutable evidence.

CASTOGAN: There is a plot to bring us all down.

SAMEDI: It must be stopped.

CASTOGAN: It will be stopped.

SAMEDI: And one of you is lying.

Beat.

LILLY: Well it's him, he's the one who's lying.

CASTOGAN: YES.

SAMEDI: No.

COOPER: *(Taken aback.)* NO, what? No! I'm not…she's lying!

LILLY: I'm not!

CASTOGAN: You're lying, you're the liar, you're pathetic, you
make me sick.

SAMEDI: CASTOGAN!

COOPER: *(Shocked.)* What?

CASTOGAN: He's a liar!

SAMEDI: Castogan!

Beat.

SAMEDI grabs CASTOGAN and stares at him. They then stare at COOPER and LILLY. SAMEDI then grabs CASTOGAN and takes him outside.

Beat.

COOPER and LILLY turn to each other, they shout in hushed whispers, with urgency.

COOPER: What the hell are you doing?

LILLY: Protecting myself.

COOPER: Protecting yourself… What? What about me?

LILLY: You seem to be doing a good enough job of that yourself.

COOPER: What? What are you talking about? Why are you telling them I'm a liar.

LILLY: Why are you telling them I'm a terrorist!

COOPER: What?

LILLY: You told them I was involved.

COOPER: I didn't.

LILLY: Don't lie to me Cooper, not any more, I know what you've been doing.

COOPER: Lilly what the hell are you talking about?

LILLY: The picture.

COOPER: Lilly I had nothing to do with the picture

LILLY: You're lying to me.

COOPER: I'm not.

LILLY: You're a liar!

COOPER: Lilly I am not lying!

LILLY: LIAR!

COOPER looks into her eyes.

COOPER: Lilly, today is the first time I've seen the picture, I swear to you on our son's life.

They stare at each other, COOPER looks away, he thinks. There is a long pause.

COOPER: Lilly I need you to be totally honest with me... Did you make the picture?

LILLY: What?

COOPER: Just tell me the truth. I can't protect you if I can't trust you.

LILLY: What?

COOPER: Promise me?

LILLY: Cooper!

COOPER: I need to know.

LILLY: I did not make that picture Cooper!

Beat, COOPER sits back, they both take a moment.

COOPER: Then it's true.

LILLY: What?

COOPER: Our son Lilly, our son. Our son made the picture.

LILLY: No, no that's not possible.

COOPER: It's the only explanation Lilly.

Beat.

LILLY: But...he's just a child.

Beat – long pause.

LILLY: How could we not have known?

COOPER: So you didn't know?

LILLY: NO! ...and you didn't?

COOPER: NO!

LILLY: How could we not have known.

COOPER: We've created a monster.

LILLY: I'm a terrible mother.

COOPER: Yes.

LILLY: Our son, our little baby boy.

COOPER: An enemy of the people.

LILLY: It breaks my heart.

COOPER: A parent's worst nightmare.

Beat.

LILLY: So what do we do?

COOPER: Well he's not taking me down with him.

LILLY: Well me neither.

COOPER: It's treason. High treason do you know what the punishment for that is? They will kill us.

LILLY: Yes.

COOPER: We have to give him up.

LILLY: What?

COOPER: We have to give them what they want.

Beat, COOPER looks around conspirationally.

COOPER: ...Look, if you back me up I think I can get us out of this. Samedi, he's the one in charge, I think he trusts me, he thinks...

LILLY: What?

COOPER: He thinks I made the picture.

LILLY: What?

COOPER: He says he wants to help me, he thinks I'm some sort of prophet, a saviour, he wants to get me out of here. If I go along with it, tell him that I made the picture, and that you helped me...

LILLY: Are you insane?

COOPER: No, he can get us out of here...

LILLY: It's a trick Cooper, he's trying to trick you, to get you to confess.

COOPER: What? But...

LILLY: Think about it, of course it is. All they want is a confession. They'll do whatever they need to get it, that's how these people work.

COOPER thinks about this for a second.

COOPER: Yes, yes of course, of course…you're right.

LILLY: You can't let them fool you Cooper.

COOPER: No

LILLY: You have to deny it, tell him you made a mistake.

COOPER: Right, you're right…

LILLY: We have each other, we can get ourselves out of this.

COOPER: Yes, yes…if we stick together, cover for each other, you scratch my back, I'll scratch yours…we can get ourselves out of this.

LILLY: We're innocent Cooper.

COOPER: Yes innocent, we're the innocents in all this, we've done nothing wrong.

LILLY: We just need to stick together.

COOPER: Yes, stick together, if we both stick to the same story, if we both tell them that neither of us knew anything about it. That we are both innocent, if we vouch for each other, cover for each other…there's nothing they can do.

LILLY: Right!

COOPER: But we have to be strong.

LILLY: Right.

COOPER: We have to stick to it.

LILLY: Right.

COOPER: Stick to our story.

LILLY: Of course.

COOPER: No matter what they do or say.

LILLY: Yes.

COOPER: Because they'll try and trick us.

LILLY: Yes they will.

COOPER: They'll try anything.

LILLY: Yes.

COOPER: Say anything.

LILLY: Yes.

COOPER: Trick us into saying things we shouldn't.

LILLY: Into incriminating ourselves.

COOPER: Or each other.

LILLY: Right and we mustn't do that.

COOPER: No, we have to stick together... Let the boy take the fall...

Beat – there is a long pause.

LILLY: ...It doesn't seem right.

COOPER: He's a terrorist Lilly! He wants to kill me, us, it's in our genes, his genes. It's textbook.

Beat.

COOPER: It's the only way.

Beat.

LILLY: I'm scared.

COOPER: Don't be, just stick to the story and we can't go wrong. I know nothing, you know nothing, right?

Beat.

LILLY: ...I love you.

Blackout

10.

We are sideways on, we see the previous scene, LILLY and COOPER are in the interrogation room talking. CASTOGAN and SAMEDI stand in the hallway talking.

SAMEDI: What the hell are you doing?

CASTOGAN: He's lying!

SAMEDI: Castogan!

CASTOGAN: Blaming his wife and child!

SAMEDI: CASTOGAN!

CASTOGAN: It's him Samedi, it's him, I'm sure of it.

SAMEDI: Castogan look at me, look at me. You have a job to do, don't you forget that.

CASTOGAN: Yes but…

SAMEDI: Castogan…

Beat.

SAMEDI: Don't think I haven't noticed… Don't you think I haven't seen it Castogan.

CASTOGAN: I don't know what you're…

SAMEDI: You are an impartial observer, independent, unbiased, detached. Your job is to find the truth. The truth Castogan. Don't be swayed, don't lose sight, don't take sides, take your eyes off the prize, don't let her manipulate you, control you, don't let it happen Castogan… What did I tell you? What did I say?

CASTOGAN: I…

SAMEDI: …Keep your wits about you, keep focused, that's what I said, keep focused Castogan, focused on the job, the job in hand. You want to do a professional job don't you?

CASTOGAN: Of course.

SAMEDI: You want to be a professional don't you?

CASTOGAN: Yes.

SAMEDI: Then act like a professional Castogan. Think like a professional…

SAMEDI stares at CASTOGAN, CASTOGAN stares back uncomfortably. He settles himself, pulls himself together.

CASTOGAN: What are you thinking?

Beat.

SAMEDI: I don't trust them.

CASTOGAN: Which one?

SAMEDI: Either of them.

CASTOGAN: Oh

SAMEDI: They'd both sacrifice the other to save themselves.

CASTOGAN: …Yes.

SAMEDI: That's an act of desperation.

CASTOGAN: It's an instinct…to survive.

SAMEDI: No, they're hiding something.

CASTOGAN: So one of them is lying?

SAMEDI: Or both. The guilty one is obviously blaming the innocent one to save themselves but the innocent one may also be blaming the guilty one to save *themselves*, not knowing the guilty one is guilty, therefore they're still lying, even though they're telling the truth. Alternatively they could both be innocent and both be blaming each other assuming that, because *they* are innocent, the other one must be guilty, even though they're not, which would mean that they're both telling the truth, even though they're both lying.

CASTOGAN: Unless the guilty one is blaming the innocent one to save themselves and the innocent one is blaming the guilty one because she knows the guilty one is guilty.

Beat, SAMEDI thinks hard.

SAMEDI: Unless…

SAMEDI thinks for a second.

The focus shifts back onto COOPER and LILLY.

LILLY: …I love you.

CASTOGAN opens the door of the room, he and SAMEDI walk in. They sit down and stare at COOPER and LILLY. After a moment, COOPER breaks the silence, LILLY looks uncomfortable.

COOPER: We've been thinking and we both realised that we were tricked. The boy manipulated us, tricked us both. He's been playing with us, toying with us. It was him who drew the picture. Neither of us knew anything about it. We are innocent, he's the one you're after. We will co-operate fully.

SAMEDI stares at COOPER, slightly taken aback. CASTOGAN watches SAMEDI. SAMEDI stares at COOPER.

SAMEDI: What?

CASTOGAN: What? No, Lilly...

SAMEDI: Cooper, you've already...

COOPER: *(Forcefully.)* I didn't make that picture!

SAMEDI stares at COOPER, he stares back.

SAMEDI: What are you telling me?

LILLY: He's saying we're innocent, that we don't know anything about the picture.

CASTOGAN: Lilly, you don't have to lie for him.

Beat.

COOPER: She's not!

SAMEDI: Is that what you're saying Cooper?

CASTOGAN: LILLY!

SAMEDI: Castogan! Cooper, is that what you're saying?

COOPER stares at SAMEDI, not knowing what to say.

COOPER: ...I'm innocent.

LILLY: We're innocent.

SAMEDI stares at COOPER. COOPER stares back. SAMEDI thinks for a moment, then looks at LILLY.

SAMEDI: Castogan, take her back to her room, I'll be in in a second.

CASTOGAN stares at SAMEDI, LILLY and COOPER look at each other nervously, COOPER nods supportively. CASTOGAN takes LILLY's arm and moves her back into her room. SAMEDI stares at COOPER. LILLY and CASTOGAN enter the second room.

SAMEDI: What are you doing?

CASTOGAN: Why are you doing this?

SAMEDI: I can't help you unless you stick to the story.

CASTOGAN: Why are you defending him?

LILLY stares at CASTOGAN, COOPER stares at SAMEDI.

SAMEDI and CASTOGAN are confused, they move slowly to the corridor. SAMEDI and CASTOGAN look at each other, they say nothing, they move into the separate rooms. SAMEDI to LILLY, CASTOGAN to COOPER.

The next two separate scenes between SAMEDI and LILLY and COOPER and CASTOGAN take place simultaniously, picking up on sentences from the two separate conversations. SAMEDI and CASTOGAN both start the tape recorders.

SAMEDI: So...

CASTOGAN: Cooper.

SAMEDI: Lilly... What's going on?

COOPER: I just told you neither of us know anything.

LILLY: We're innocent.

CASTOGAN: Is that right?

COOPER: Yes.

SAMEDI: You're both innocent?

LILLY: YES!

CASTOGAN: And you'd swear to that?

COOPER: Yes...

SAMEDI and CASTOGAN sit back in their chairs.

SAMEDI: ...And your son made the picture?

CASTOGAN: Your son is the guilty one?

COOPER: Yes.

SAMEDI: ...you're prepared to let him take the fall for this?

CASTOGAN: Your four-year-old boy?

SAMEDI: You do know what the punishment for this is?

COOPER: He made the picture.

SAMEDI: You'd really let him die? Your baby boy?

CASTOGAN: You're lying.

SAMEDI: Why Lilly? To save yourself? To save your husband? Or because you know it's true, because you know he's guilty?

LILLY stares at SAMEDI.

COOPER: He's guilty.

Beat.

SAMEDI: What did he say to you?

CASTOGAN: What did you say to her?

LILLY: Nothing.

COOPER: I didn't say anything.

SAMEDI: What game are you playing here Lilly?

LILLY: I'm not playing a game.

CASTOGAN: I know you did it.

COOPER: What?

SAMEDI: Who made this picture?

LILLY: I don't know.

COOPER: My son made the picture.

SAMEDI: I thought you said your son made the picture?

LILLY: No.

CASTOGAN: You really expect me to believe that your son made that picture.

COOPER: Yes.

LILLY: ...I don't know.

SAMEDI: Lilly listen to me, you do not understand how important this is.

CASTOGAN: You're a liar!

SAMEDI: I need to know who made this picture!

COOPER: I didn't make the picture.

LILLY: I don't know who made the picture.

CASTOGAN: You could save her…

SAMEDI: I'm going to give you a choice Lilly.

CASTOGAN: …and your son, you could save them both.

SAMEDI: You can save one of them Lilly.

CASTOGAN: Just admit it, tell the truth.

SAMEDI: Tell me who made the picture.

CASTOGAN: Tell me you made the picture.

COOPER: I did not make the picture.

CASTOGAN burns with frustration. He takes out a cigarette and lights it. He smokes, remaining silent. COOPER watches him. SAMEDI turns off his tape recorder, CASTOGAN does not.

SAMEDI: All I want is the truth Lilly…the person who made that picture Lilly, I want to help them, I swear to you. No lies, no games, I'm risking my job, my life by telling you this. It's the truth… You've seen it Lilly, you've seen the picture, what it is, what it means, this is more important than any of us Lilly, bigger than you, or me, or your husband. We need to preserve it's creator Lilly, we need to save them, you and I can do that together. You just need to tell me who made the picture…

LILLY stares at him.

LILLY: No, you're trying to trick me.

SAMEDI: No Lilly, no games, no tricks.

LILLY: You're trying to get me to say something I shouldn't.

SAMEDI: Just tell me the truth.

LILLY: I don't know the truth…

Beat.

SAMEDI: Your husband told me he made it.

LILLY stares at him.

SAMEDI: He asked me to save him Lilly, to let you and your son die and to save himself.

LILLY: You're lying.

SAMEDI: Maybe I am, you have no way of knowing, one way or the other I know you know who made this picture. You can save one of them.

LILLY: Please...

CASTOGAN: I'm going to give you one more chance.

SAMEDI: Do you believe your son made this picture?

CASTOGAN: Did you make this picture?

LILLY: I believe my husband did not make it.

COOPER: I didn't make the picture.

Beat.

SAMEDI stares at LILLY, CASTOGAN stares at COOPER.

SAMEDI: OK, that's good enough for me.

SAMEDI stands, he exits, he walks into the corridor. He stares at his picture, he tries to clear his head, he looks through the spyhole to the room where COOPER and CASTOGAN sit. He looks back to the picture. Takes a moment. After a long beat he starts to laugh and shakes his head.

SAMEDI: It's the boy!

CASTOGAN is still smoking silently. SAMEDI puts the picture into his pocket and knocks on the door, CASTOGAN puts out the cigarette, stands and exits into the corridor.

CASTOGAN: Well?

SAMEDI: ...She's guilty.

CASTOGAN: What?

SAMEDI: They both are.

CASTOGAN: Are you sure?

SAMEDI: Positive.

CASTOGAN: But...she can't be.

SAMEDI: Her and the husband…in it together. The child's the innocent in all of this.

CASTOGAN: The child? But?

SAMEDI: Think about it Castogan, we leave them alone for five minutes and now suddenly their stories match? Sticking together like boiled bones. Why do you think they are both so keen to pin it on the child? They're trying to save themselves? They're conspirators. It's textbook.

CASTOGAN: But…

SAMEDI: They have one purpose, one desire and they are prepared to sacrifice anything, including their very own child to carry it out. Textbook.

CASTOGAN: But she seems so lovely.

SAMEDI: I know Castogan I know.

CASTOGAN: I just can't believe it.

SAMEDI: Then see for yourself. Go in there…push her…no matter what you say she'll say the same thing, that she and him are innocent, that it's the child to blame… Try it, see for yourself.

CASTOGAN: And what if she is?

SAMEDI: You know the orders, Castogan.

CASTOGAN stares at SAMEDI, SAMEDI nods to the door. After a moment CASTOGAN enters LILLY's room. SAMEDI watches, he then gets the picture out of his pocket and stares at it. He looks through the spyhole at CASTOGAN and LILLY, then through the spyhole at COOPER. He goes back to the picture, then enters COOPER's room. The two scenes take place siumltaniously again. SAMEDI looks down at the cigarette butt in front of COOPER. CASTOGAN turns on his tape recorder, SAMEDI turns his off.

CASTOGAN: What's going on Lilly?

LILLY: Please…

COOPER: I'm innocent.

CASTOGAN: Why are you doing this?

LILLY: I haven't done anything.

COOPER: I just want to get out of here, please…

CASTOGAN: Please Lilly, just tell me the truth I can help you.

COOPER: What you said before, about getting me out…it was a trick wasn't it?

LILLY: We're innocent.

Beat.

COOPER: I'm innocent.

Beat – CASTOGAN and SAMEDI stare at LILLY and COOPER.

CASTOGAN: I could have helped you Lilly.

SAMEDI: I could have saved you.

LILLY: I'm sorry.

COOPER: What?

CASTOGAN: I wanted to help you.

CASTOGAN stares at LILLY, SAMEDI stares at COOPER.

CASTOGAN: I'm sorry.

CASTOGAN and SAMEDI walk over to the desk, CASTOGAN turns off his tape recorder, SAMEDI puts the picture into his pocket. They sigh, roll up their sleeves and slowly pull out the black hoods, COOPER and LILLY do not see this. CASTOGAN looks very pained. They slowly walk around behind LILLY and COOPER.

CASTOGAN: I'm going to take you home now Lilly.

SAMEDI: I'm going to take good care of your son.

LILLY: Really?

CASTOGAN: Yes…

COOPER: My son?

LILLY: What about my son?

CASTOGAN stares down at the black hood.

CASTOGAN: I really like you Lilly.

LILLY: Thank you.

CASTOGAN and SAMEDI stand behind LILLY and COOPER, holding the hoods.

Blackout.

11.

SAMEDI and CASTOGAN sit in one of the interrogation rooms, they don't speak. For a long long time.

SAMEDI: Give me a cigarette.

CASTOGAN: Samedi?

SAMEDI: Give me a cigarette, I have a spare five minutes.

SAMEDI takes the cigarette packet and lights one. CASTOGAN watches him. He looks upset.

Beat.

CASTOGAN: When will it be done?

SAMEDI: Soon.

CASTOGAN sighs.

CASTOGAN: Will they let me say goodbye?

SAMEDI stares at CASTOGAN, after a moment he offers him a cigarette. CASTOGAN looks confused, then nervously takes one. SAMEDI reaches in to light the cigarette, he stares at CASTOGAN affectionately, he strokes his face.

SAMEDI: I will miss you Castogan.

CASTOGAN smiles at the compliment, but he is confused.

CASTOGAN: Miss me?

SAMEDI looks at him, then moves away, they smoke the rest of their cigarettes.

SAMEDI: Where is the boy?

CASTOGAN: He's on his way. What will happen to him…after his parents are…?

SAMEDI: He'll be put into care. I've volunteered to look after him in the meantime.

CASTOGAN: Really. God Samedi, what a wonderful gesture.

SAMEDI: What can I say, I'm a kind man with a big heart.

CASTOGAN: You are Samedi, you are.

Beat.

SAMEDI: Go and check on him.

CASTOGAN: What?

SAMEDI: The boy. See if he's arrived yet.

CASTOGAN: Right. Yes, of course…

CASTOGAN gets up to leave, as he gets to the door he stops.

CASTOGAN: She was lovely Samedi wasn't she…? Lilly?

SAMEDI: Yes Castogan, yes she was.

CASTOGAN: Pretty as a picture.

CASTOGAN smiles mournfully and exits. SAMEDI remains still for a moment then checks to see that CASTOGAN has gone. He turns his attentions to the tape recorder, he rewinds it and presses play, we hear a few various titbits from the interviews. He continues to rewind it until we hear…

(On Tape.)

COOPER: Today is the first time I've seen the picture, I swear to you on our son's life.

There is a long pause.

COOPER: Lilly I need you to be totally honest with me… Did you make the picture?

LILLY: What? No!

COOPER: Just tell me the truth. I can't protect you if I can't trust you.

LILLY: What?

COOPER: Promise me?

LILLY: Cooper!

COOPER: I need to know.

LILLY: I did not make that picture Cooper!

Beat.

COOPER: Then it's true.

LILLY: What?

COOPER: Our son Lilly, our son. Our son made the picture.

LILLY: No, no that's not possible.

COOPER: It's the only explanation Lilly.

Beat.

LILLY: But he's just a child.

SAMEDI stops the tape recorder and ejects the tape, he looks at it for a moment, he then breaks it in two and rips all the tape out of the cassette. He then puts the destroyed tape into his pocket.

A moment later CASTOGAN opens the door.

CASTOGAN: He's here Samedi, the boy's here.

SAMEDI: Excellent… Bring him in.

Blackout.

12.

We remain in blackout, we hear a tape recording play. There is the voice of a four-year-old boy.

BOY: So you found the picture?

SAMEDI: Yes…

BOY: Well…?

SAMEDI: What does it mean?

BOY: What do you want it to mean?

SAMEDI: …I don't know.

BOY: What do you think it means?

SAMEDI: I… I'm not sure…

BOY: Think harder.

Beat.

The tape recorder stops.

End.